FRIENDS
OF ACPL

Living with the Weather

RAIN, WIND AND STORM

Nicola Baxter

RSVP

**RAINTREE
STECK-VAUGHN**
P U B L I S H E R S
The Steck-Vaughn Company

Austin, Texas

Other books in the series

FOG, MIST AND SMOG
HEAT AND DROUGHT
SNOW AND ICE

Published by Raintree Steck-Vaughn Publishers,
an imprint of Steck-Vaughn Company

Library of Congress Cataloging-in-Publication Data
Baxter, Nicola.
Rain, Wind and Storm / Nicola Baxter.
    p.   cm.—(Living with weather)
    Includes bibliographical references and index.
    Summary: Describes different kinds of storms, their causes,
    the damage they can inflict, and ways of dealing with them.
    ISBN 0-8172-5050-6
    1. Storms—Juvenile literature.
    2. Weather—Juvenile literature.
    [1. Storms.]
    I. Title. II. Series.
    QC941.3.B39   1998
    551.55—dc21   97-8063

Printed in Italy. Bound in the United States.
1 2 3 4 5 6 7 8 9 0 02 01 00 99 98

CONTENTS

A STORMY START

Somewhere in the world, right this minute, rain is streaming down over fields and factories. High winds are tossing tiles from rooftops. People are fumbling for candles in the dark after a storm has cut off the electricity. All of us have known weather something like this. It's not surprising that stories about wild weather, even from ancient times, are part of our lives today.

Weather Wonders

In early times, no one knew what caused rain, wind, and storms. Bad weather could only mean that the gods were angry. The Bible tells of forty days of rain, leading to a massive flood, when God was unhappy with human behavior. Scandinavian myths show the god Thor, thundering across the sky, throwing fearsome lightning bolts.

Riding the Whirlwind

The Wizard of Oz by Frank L. Baum tells how Dorothy is blown away to a magical land by a tornado:

> There came a great shriek from the wind, and the house shook so hard that she lost her footing.... The house whirled around two or three times and rose slowly through the air.

▼ In the modern world, we often feel that we are in control of most parts of our lives. But the weather can still surprise and challenge us.

WEATHER TODAY

Mackerel sky, mackerel sky,
Maybe wet, maybe dry.

Will it be nice enough for a picnic a week from next Tuesday? In a few parts of the world, the weather is so predictable that you can make plans quite safely. But on most of our planet, the weather is changeable. There may be rain, wind, or storms. That is because, high above us, the atmosphere of the earth is always on the move.

Weather Matters

We seem to talk about the weather a lot, but does it really matter? After all, we are usually safe and warm inside our homes and cars. In fact, the weather matters to everyone, and not just when we decide what to wear in the morning. But there is a big difference between a small thunderstorm, bringing welcome water to crops and reservoirs, and a massive hurricane, destroying homes and property. However, with modern technology, we are able to understand and prepare for most kinds of weather better than ever before.

▶ Modern materials, such as plastics, can protect us from the weather, as these Guatemalan boys have found. Their soccer game will probably have to be postponed.

▼ Once, lightning was the brightest thing to light up a night sky. Now, we are used to electric lights, so lightning seems less startling.

▲ Even in areas where violent storms are common, it is hard to prepare fully for them. When drains and water systems cannot cope with the amount of rain that falls, flooding harms people and property.

THE WILDEST WEATHER

How often have you complained that the weather is too wet or too windy? But too little rain or wind is as bad as too much. It can be a disaster when not enough rain falls to keep crops alive and to supply enough water for families and factories. It is having more or less rain than usual that causes difficulty. Often we can plan for the weather we expect, but unexpected weather conditions cause problems.

Storm Drill

At school you practice what to do if there is a fire. But do you practice what to do if a violent storm strikes? Some children do. They live in what is known as the "hurricane belt," where fierce winds and lashing rain can strike at certain seasons. It is impossible to keep all buildings and property safe, but these children can learn where they should shelter to protect themselves from harm during a hurricane.

WEATHER WORDS

★ The words rain, wind, and storm are not the only ones we use to describe different kinds of weather. There are lots of other words, such as downpour, drizzle, breeze, and gale. Some expressions are quite strange. We say it rains cats and dogs, the French say it rains pitchforks, and the Germans say that it rains rivers.

◀ Rain in a city may seem annoying, but it fills reservoirs and rivers and washes away dust and dirt.

WHAT CAUSES WEATHER

There is no air in space. Astronauts cannot breathe without oxygen tanks. But our planet is surrounded by a deep layer of gas, called atmosphere. The atmosphere of earth is over 600 mi. (1,000 km) deep, but it is only the lower level, called the troposphere, that has breathable air.

THE WEATHER LAYER

Our planet's weather happens in the troposphere. The atmosphere is pressing down on the earth all the time. This atmospheric pressure is greater in some places than in others. Where the air is warm, it rises, putting less pressure on the earth beneath. Cold air sinks, causing greater pressure. Atmospheric pressure is measured with a barometer.

WHAT A GAS!

The troposphere stretches up for 6 to 12 mi. (10 to 20 km). It is almost twice as deep above the equator as it is above the North and South poles. The air is made up of about 78 percent nitrogen, 21 percent oxygen, and small amounts of other gases.

▲ The earth's heat comes from the sun. The equator is the part of the earth nearest the sun. The sun's rays heat it directly. At the poles, the sun's rays are at an angle to the earth, so the heat is spread out and the poles are much cooler.

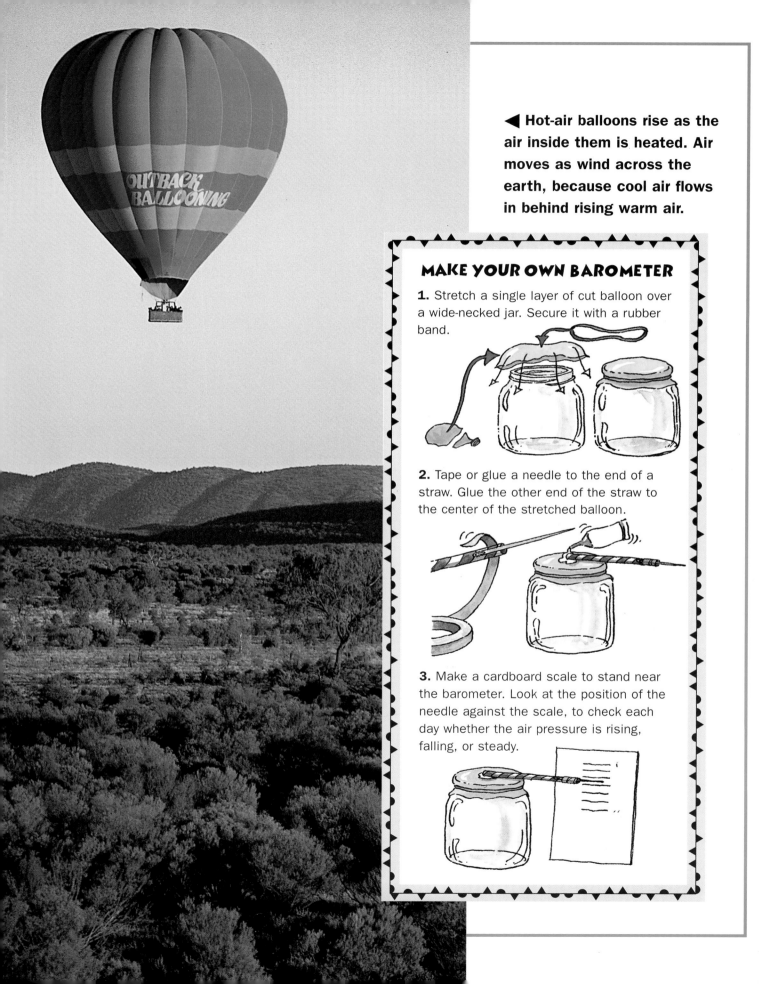

◀ Hot-air balloons rise as the air inside them is heated. Air moves as wind across the earth, because cool air flows in behind rising warm air.

MAKE YOUR OWN BAROMETER

1. Stretch a single layer of cut balloon over a wide-necked jar. Secure it with a rubber band.

2. Tape or glue a needle to the end of a straw. Glue the other end of the straw to the center of the stretched balloon.

3. Make a cardboard scale to stand near the barometer. Look at the position of the needle against the scale, to check each day whether the air pressure is rising, falling, or steady.

WEATHER TRENDS

The general weather trends of an area are known as its climate. Weather is what happens from day to day. The earth is like a ball, spinning in space as it travels once a year around the sun. Because the earth is tilted, some places are nearer to the sun at one time of the year than at another. This causes the change of seasons. Although weather on Earth can vary a great deal from day to day, we can tell which areas are most likely to experience certain kinds of weather and at what time of the year they are most likely to happen.

▲ The rainy season in Bali lasts from May to October. This boy is used to getting wet on his way to school.

Blowing and Flowing

In most parts of the world, there are winds that tend to blow from a particular direction all the time. These are called prevailing winds. They affect how much rain places have, as they blow clouds from one area to another. Some parts of the world have very heavy rainy seasons, called monsoons.

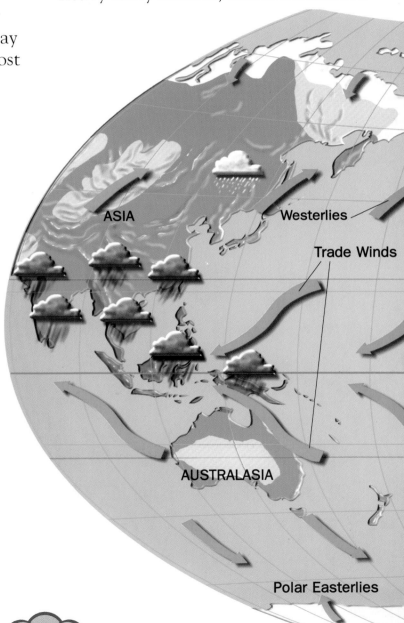

ASIA

Westerlies

Trade Winds

AUSTRALASIA

Polar Easterlies

12

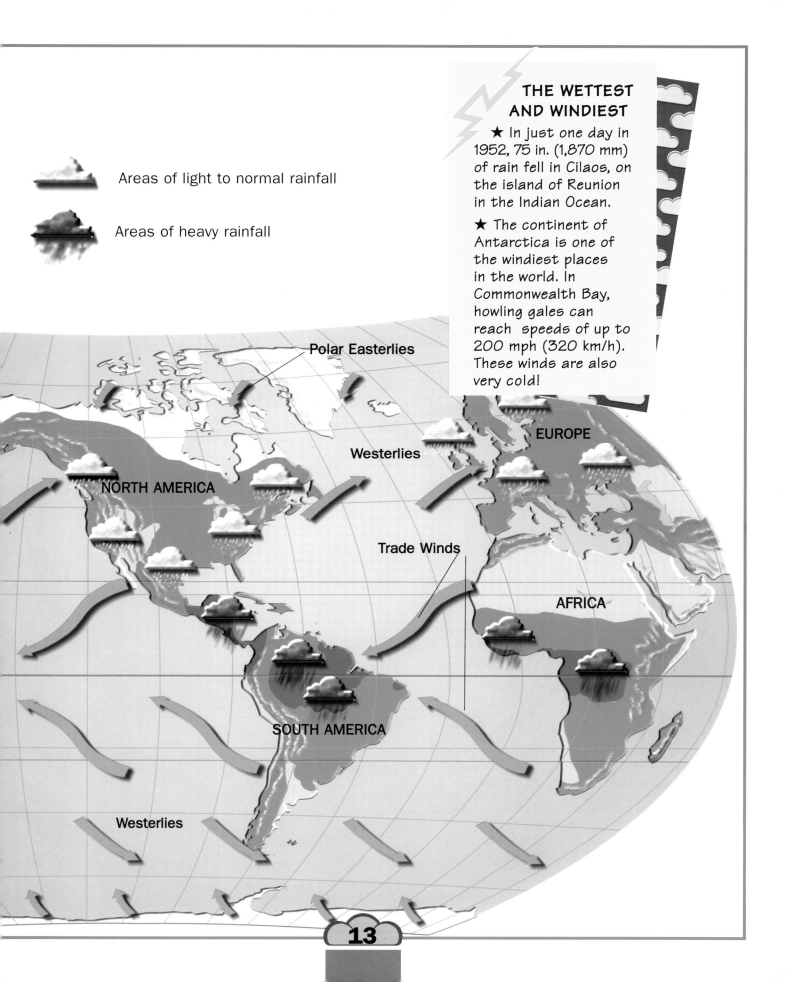

Areas of light to normal rainfall

Areas of heavy rainfall

THE WETTEST AND WINDIEST

★ In just one day in 1952, 75 in. (1,870 mm) of rain fell in Cilaos, on the island of Reunion in the Indian Ocean.

★ The continent of Antarctica is one of the windiest places in the world. In Commonwealth Bay, howling gales can reach speeds of up to 200 mph (320 km/h). These winds are also very cold!

Polar Easterlies

Westerlies

EUROPE

NORTH AMERICA

Trade Winds

AFRICA

SOUTH AMERICA

Westerlies

WINDY WEATHER
What Is Wind?

Wind is simply air that is on the move. Differences in temperature and atmospheric pressure make air move from place to place. It moves from high pressure areas to low-pressure areas. Areas of high pressure are called anticyclones. They are caused when cool air sinks. Warm, rising air causes low pressure areas, called depressions or cyclones. Air tries to flow directly from areas of high pressure to areas of low pressure, but the winds are pushed off course by the earth's spin.

The Jet Stream

At ground level, moving air may be felt as the lightest breeze or the fiercest gale, but at the top of the troposphere there are winds, too. The jet stream is a very strong wind, traveling at more than 125 mph (200 km/h); it can blow for very long distances.

Hurricanes blow from the Caribbean Sea toward the land and up the east coast of North America.

Hurricanes blow along the west coast of the Americas from May to November.

FAST TRACK

★ A strong jet stream across the Atlantic Ocean affects the amount of time it takes to fly between the United States and Europe. Airplanes can take as much as an hour longer to cross the Atlantic in a westerly direction than they do in an easterly one.

◄ Storm winds that blow regularly are often given special names. Violent storms are called hurricanes in the Caribbean, typhoons in the China Seas, willy-willies near Australia, and cyclones in the Indian Ocean.

How Windy Is It?

At sea, where strong winds can whip up waves large enough to smash a ship to pieces, it is especially important to be accurate when describing winds. So in 1806 a British admiral, Sir Francis Beaufort, devised a scale for describing the force of the wind.

The Beaufort Scale

0	Calm	less than 1 mph (1 km/h)
1	Light air	1–3 mph (1–5 km/h)
2	Light breeze	4–7 mph (6–11 km/h)
3	Gentle breeze	8–12 mph (12–19 km/h)
4	Moderate breeze	13–18 mph (20–29 km/h)
5	Fresh breeze	19–24 mph (30–39 km/h)
6	Strong breeze	25–31 mph (40–50 km/h)
7	Near gale	32–38 mph (51–61 km/h)
8	Gale	39–46 mph (62–74 km/h)
9	Severe gale	47–54 mph (75–87 km/h)
10	Storm	55–63 mph (88–101 km/h)
11	Severe storm	64–72 mph (102–117 km/h)
12	Hurricane	over 72 mph (118 km/h)

▶ **Winds do not always mean danger. This windsurfer in Alaska is making full use of them for fun.**

WEATHER FRONTS

Putting a cup of coffee outside will make the air above it warm and cause it to rise, but it will not affect the weather! It is huge warm and cool air masses, causing high and low pressure areas, that do so. Where a warm and cold air mass meet is called a front. It is usually along these fronts, as they move over land and sea, that weather changes tend to happen.

Land and Sea Breezes

In hot weather, land and sea breezes blow along the coast. Under sunshine, the land heats up faster than the sea, so warm air rises from the land, forming an area of low pressure. Cooler air moves from above the sea to replace the rising warm air. This causes a sea breeze. At night, the land quickly becomes cooler than the sea. Cool air moves in to replace the warmer, rising air above the sea, and creates a land breeze.

▼ Hurricane winds blow at more than 150 mph (240 km/h). They usually happen in summer or fall, when the seas are warm.

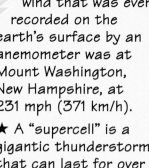

Wind Words

Winds are described by the direction from which they are blowing. An east wind, for example, blows from the east. A northwesterly blows from the north-west. Wind speed is measured by using an instrument called an anemometer.

MAKE YOUR OWN ANEMOMETER

1. Glue two narrow 12 in.-(30 cm-) long pieces of balsa wood together in the middle to form a cross.

2. Glue a clean plastic cup or carton to the end of each arm, so that each is pointing in the same direction. One cup should be a different color from the rest.

3. Nail through the center of the wooden cross into a post, putting beads above and below the cross and making sure that the anemometer turns freely.

4. Place the anemometer in an open spot. As the wind blows, see how fast the colored cup goes around. Look again a few hours later. Is the wind stronger, or has it died down?

THE WATER CYCLE

Without water, there could be no life on Earth. Water on Earth is always on the move, rising into the air as invisible water vapor and falling again as rain, hail, or snow. This rising and falling is known as the water cycle. The amount of water on Earth does not change, but it moves constantly from place to place.

How Clouds Are Formed

The sun's heat makes water evaporate—or turn into vapor—and rise into the air. As it rises higher, the vapor cools and turns back into millions of liquid droplets, forming clouds. The air is even colder where the highest clouds form, so the droplets turn into ice crystals—solid water. When the water or ice crystals become too large, they fall as rain, snow, or hail.

WATERWORLD

★ It is a bit misleading to call our planet "earth." Over two-thirds (71 percent) of the planet is covered by water. Living things cannot survive without it. The oceans contain 97 percent of all the world's water.

★ A raindrop is shaped like a flattened ball. It is not perfectly round nor is it shaped like a teardrop.

Water vapor forms into clouds, which are blown along by the wind.

As the sun heats the ocean, warm air rises, carrying water vapor with it.

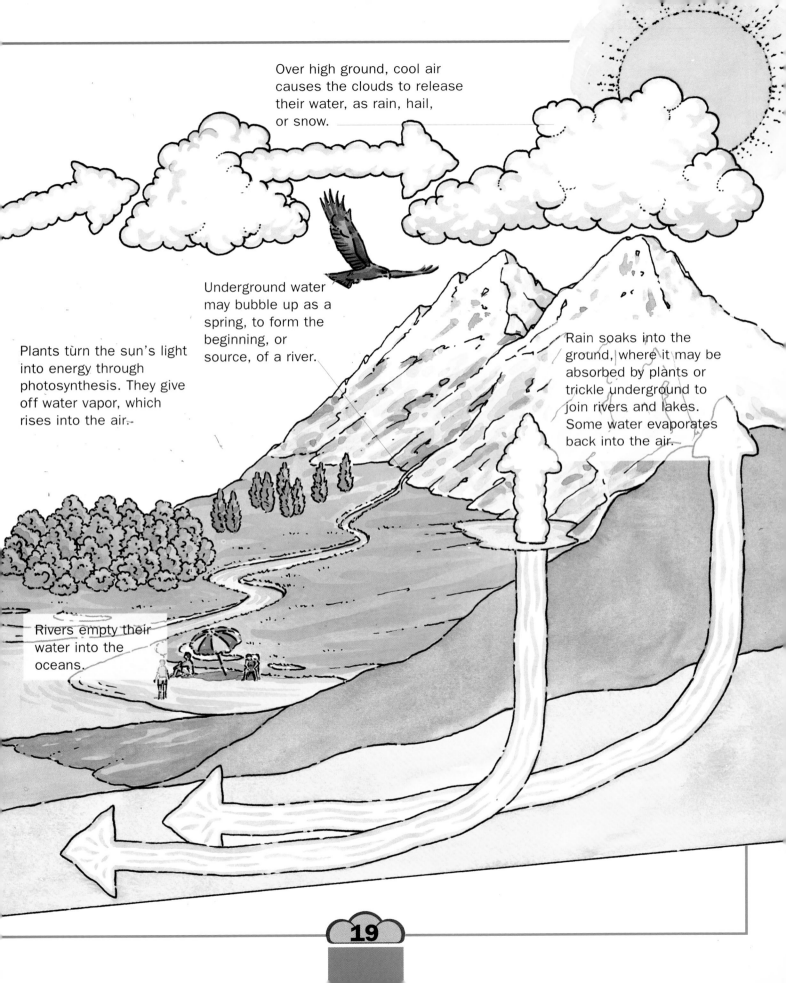

Over high ground, cool air causes the clouds to release their water, as rain, hail, or snow.

Underground water may bubble up as a spring, to form the beginning, or source, of a river.

Plants turn the sun's light into energy through photosynthesis. They give off water vapor, which rises into the air.

Rain soaks into the ground, where it may be absorbed by plants or trickle underground to join rivers and lakes. Some water evaporates back into the air.

Rivers empty their water into the oceans.

CLOUD CLUES

Weather watchers can learn a great deal from clouds. A "mackerel sky" (called cirrocumulus, meaning "feathery heaps"), for example, may warn of unsettled weather to come. But it is the massive cumulonimbus clouds ("rainbearing heaps") that bring heavy thunderstorms, while lower, flatter nimbostratus clouds ("rainbearing layers") bring drizzle or showers.

▼ **Air cools as it rises, which is why water vapor often condenses into cumulus clouds above high ground.**

▼ **Dark stratus clouds like these warn of rain or snow in the near future. However, the storm may be short-lived because there is brighter weather behind it.**

◀ Lightning flashes run down to discharge themselves and then go immediately up again along the same path. We see the upstroke as a brilliant streak in the sky.

Storm Danger

Never take shelter under a tree in a thunderstorm! The tree is actually inviting lightning to strike it. That is because the positive electrical charge in the treetop attracts the negative charge at the bottom of a storm cloud. Any tall object risks being struck by lightning in a thunderstorm.

STARTLING STORMS

★ Cumulonimbus clouds stretch up to 49,230 ft. (15,000 m), which is almost twice as high as Mount Everest.

★ New York's Empire State Building is struck by lightning as often as 500 times a year. It does not have a lightning rod!

★ Volcanic eruptions are often accompanied by lightning.

▲ Static electricity develops inside clouds, with positive charge at the top and negative charge at the bottom.

▲ The negative charge is released as an electrical spark, jumping to the nearest positively charged object, such as a tree.

WIND STORMS

HURRICANE DAMAGE

Flooding and lightning damage may accompany a heavy thunderstorm, but compared with the destructive power of a hurricane, it really is a storm in a teacup. Hurricanes, typhoons, and cyclones are all different names for fierce tropical storms.

A Summer Storm

During the summer months, tropical seas heat up, and the warm air above them rises quickly, taking moisture with it. This area of low pressure causes cooler winds to rush in underneath, whirling up around the rising air as they too become warmer. As the air rises, it cools. The water vapor in it condenses to form huge, swirling clouds. These hurricane winds swirl around at up to 200 mph (320 km/h).

◄ **A hurricane can cause extreme damage to anything in its path. Even modern buildings such as this one in Florida cannot withstand the force. Two concrete walls have been totally removed, revealing the rooms within, looking like an abandoned dollhouse.**

FLASHPOINTS

★ Researchers at the National Aeronautics and Space Administration (NASA) have discovered that at any given instant there are more than 2,000 thunderstorms taking place throughout the world. They all combine to produce about 100 lightning flashes per second, each one with the power of up to a billion volts!

★After it was devastated by a tidal wave caused by Hurricane Hattie on October 13, 1961, the capital city of Belize in Central America was moved 50 mi. (80 km) inland to a new site called Belmopan, where hurricanes can't reach.

Naming Hurricanes

Hurricanes are given names, such as Hurricane Hugo. Every year, a list is drawn up of names beginning with each letter of the alphabet. The first hurricane of the season is given a name beginning with A, the next one beginning with B, and so on. This system is over one hundred years old and was first devised by Clement Wragge, an Australian weather forecaster.

TORNADO TROUBLE

Whereas hurricanes build up over the sea, tornadoes are twisting funnels that develop over land. These violent whirlwinds form where warm, moist air meets colder, drier air flowing in from another direction. A twisting column of air stretches from the storm clouds down to the ground. Like hurricanes, they have a central area of very low pressure, around which powerful winds rush in spirals. It is not only the winds that cause damage. The low-pressure center of the tornado can also cause buildings to explode, since the pressure inside the buildings is so much greater.

▼ The powerful upward current of air in the center of a tornado sucks up anything in its path. People, animals, cars, and even buildings have been swept up by tornadoes and thrown down hundreds of feet (meters) away.

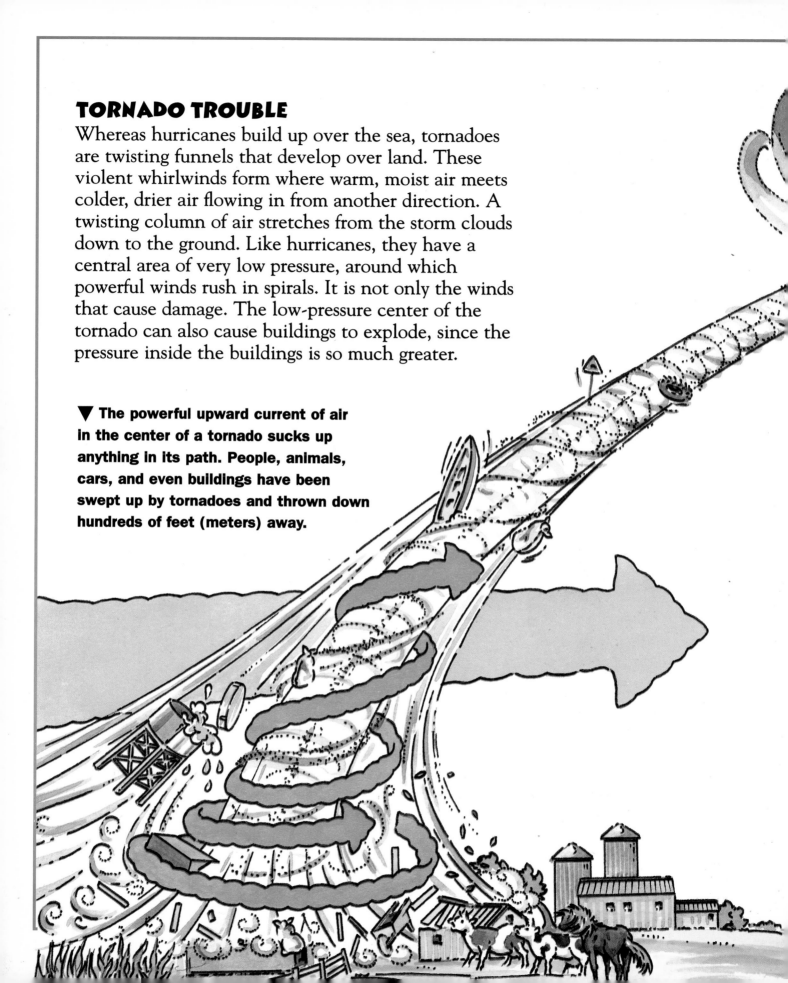

Miracle Boy

Nine-month-old Joshua Walls had a lucky escape when a tornado swept across Arkansas. He was picked up by 190 mph (300 km/h) winds and put down unharmed 900 ft. (270 m) away. "One day we will have to tell Joshua he is alive only because of a miracle," said his grandmother.

Storm Study

The path of a tornado is not completely predictable. Scientists studying tornadoes sometimes try to follow them by car, but that can be very dangerous if a tornado suddenly heads toward them! Debris sucked up by the tornado may be thrown in all directions—an added danger to nearby people and their property.

▼ A marine tornado draws seawater up into its spiraling funnel, forming a giant "water spout" clearly visible from a distance.

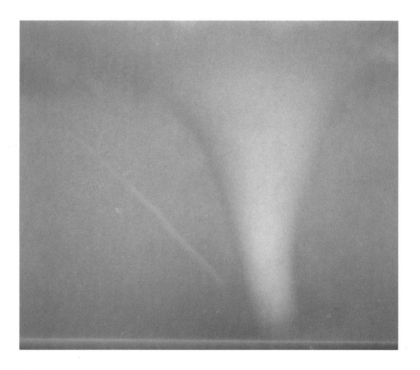

Storm Signs

Tornadoes may appear dark and menacing or resemble whirling orange pillars—it all depends on the color of the dust and dirt that the tornado has sucked up from the ground. Eventually the tornado spends some of its energy and lifts from the ground, although there is still a danger that it may touch down again to do more damage.

MAKE A MINI-TORNADO

1. Place a glass at the center of a revolving cake stand, and fasten it securely with tape.

2. Pour soda water into the glass almost to the top, leaving a small space.

3. Spin the cake stand and pour a little salt into the glass. The tiny bubbles of gas that are released will form a mini-tornado.

◀ **This tornado is whirling over Monument Valley in Arizona, luckily not a very populated area of the country. In fact, it is clear that there has been violent weather there for thousands of years, for the rocks themselves have been worn into pillars by the winds.**

Tornado Alley

Whirlwinds occur in many parts of the world, but the most violent tornadoes appear across the Great Plains of the United States. Hundreds of tornadoes can happen on the same day, whirling through the nine states known as "Tornado Alley."

Tornado Tragedy

The worst tornado ever to hit the United States was the Tri-State Tornado on March 18, 1925. Almost 700 people were killed. "The normally weatherwise farmers were apparently unaware of what was bearing down on them. With such great forward speed...the tornado gave these people too little time to react," said one report.

FLYING FROGS

★ Tornadoes can scoop up almost anything in their paths. Fantastic stories of the clouds "raining frogs" may actually be true! If a tornado has sucked up a number of the little croaking creatures and dropped them hundreds of yards (meters) from the water, it may seem as if they have rained down from the heavens!

FORECASTING RAIN

Even the most extreme storms are easier to live with if we have warning of their arrival. That is why weather forecasting is so important. The science of weather forecasting is called meteorology.

But forecasting is useless if the information cannot reach people who need to know. In isolated areas with poor communications, weather warnings can be difficult to deliver in time.

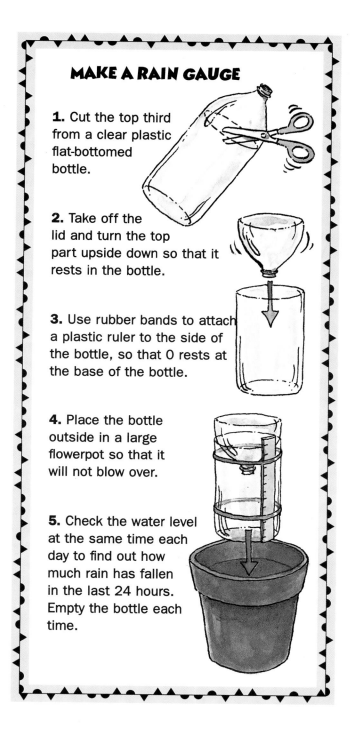

MAKE A RAIN GAUGE

1. Cut the top third from a clear plastic flat-bottomed bottle.

2. Take off the lid and turn the top part upside down so that it rests in the bottle.

3. Use rubber bands to attach a plastic ruler to the side of the bottle, so that 0 rests at the base of the bottle.

4. Place the bottle outside in a large flowerpot so that it will not blow over.

5. Check the water level at the same time each day to find out how much rain has fallen in the last 24 hours. Empty the bottle each time.

◄ **Weather forecasts are a regular feature on our television screens, telling us what kind of weather to expect.**

Weather Watchers

What weather watchers need above all is information—as much of it as possible. Weather stations on land, at sea, and on orbiting satellites all send information back to meteorological centers, where computers help to process the facts and figures about temperature, atmospheric pressure, and wind speed.

BYGONE FORECASTING

★ From the earliest times, people have tried to predict the weather.

★ In the United States it is said that if a groundhog wakes up from its winter sleep on February 2 and sees its own shadow (because it is sunny), then there will be six more weeks of winter.

★ In Great Britain, rain on St. Swithin's Day (July 15) is said to mean that it will rain for another 40 days.

★ A red sky at night is said to mean fine weather to come, while a red sky in the morning warns of cold and storms.

Weather Warnings

Regular weather forecasts are broadcast on radio and television at set times of the day and night, so that listeners know when they can receive information. Special broadcasts are made for sailors and farmers. Those needing instant, up-to-date information can also telephone special numbers or use the Internet.

LIVING WITH STORMS

CITY SURVIVAL

The weather affects everyone. But surely, in a city where there are plenty of buildings for shelter, extremes of weather are not so serious? In fact, cities have to be carefully planned and built so major problems can be avoided. After all, in a city, damage to one building or a flood over a small area can affect huge numbers of people.

Air Pollution

Cities are never still. The roads are crowded with traffic, and the air is often thick with pollution. An area of high pressure over a city means that fumes from traffic, homes, offices, and factories are trapped in the streets. In many cities, cyclists and pedestrians wear masks that filter the air they breathe.

◀ **It is easy to catch a cold or a cough in a crowded train or bus. Public transportation in the city can be a breeding ground for germs.**

▼ **These city buildings are specially designed to cope with extremes of weather.**

Some buildings are designed to bend in high winds. This prevents the structure from cracking.

Sloping roofs allow the rain to run off easily. Flat roofs need special protection from water puddles that are left after a storm.

City Plans

It is vitally important that traffic can keep moving through a city, whatever the weather. But planning for traffic creates its own problems—wide, straight streets act as wind tunnels, funneling breezes through narrow openings to create dangerous gusts and crosswinds.

Tall buildings often have lightning rods at the top, to prevent their being damaged in thunderstorms.

Rain Drains

Excellent drainage is needed to cope with rainwater, however heavily it falls, but in most places the water must not be wasted. It is piped to reservoirs to supply the city's vast need for water during dry periods. Water, especially in warmer areas, can be a serious health hazard, another reason why excess water should not be allowed to stand and stagnate.

Canopies protect people from the rain when entering buildings from the street.

PREVENTING DAMAGE

A quick look at a city's buildings and how they have been constructed can tell you a great deal about the kind of weather the city expects. Heavy window shutters indicate severe storms at certain times of the year. Buildings with wide guttering show that there is often heavy rainfall.

◄ Power outages are sometimes caused by storm damage to electricity cables. Restoring the electricity supply to a town or city is a highly skilled job and can be dangerous.

Power Supplies

A power outage can be a disaster in a city. Most heating and lighting is powered by electricity. Without street lights and traffic signals, roads quickly become chaotic. As far as possible, electricity cables are run underground, where winds and lightning cannot damage them. Hospitals and other key buildings have their own generators for emergency use.

▼ **Severe weather warnings must be given in cities that lie in the paths of hurricanes. Life goes on despite the aftereffects of a storm, as in the city of Dhaka, Bangladesh.**

Sparks and Storms

Fires are dangerous wherever they break out, but in cities a small fire can rapidly spread to destroy nearby buildings. Lightning rods help prevent fires caused by lightning strikes.

▼ **In Japan, cities such as Tokyo have computer-generated information boards that warn commuters if a storm is on its way.**

WORKING WITH THE WEATHER

People who live and work in cities find it hard enough, dashing through rain and wind to warm, dry offices. But many people live and work in the countryside. For farmers, the weather is both a friend and an enemy. They need rain—but not too much and not at the wrong time. One of the skills of farming lies in making the most of the weather, working with it and not against it.

SMELLING RAIN

★ It really is true that some people can "smell rain." During dry weather, oils from the air are trapped in the soil. Moisture in the air interacts with oils in the earth to give off a smell that we associate with wet weather.

◀ Asian farmers make the best use of their heavy rainfalls by channeling water to flood their fields, so that young rice plants can have the conditions they need to grow.

Out in All Weathers

Many workers—in farms, forests, parks, and gardens—need to be outside, whatever the weather. Besides good protective clothing, they need tractors and vans that are up to the job. Four-wheel-drive vehicles can negotiate muddy tracks, even on steep hills. Wide wheels on tractors and earth-moving equipment allow them to be used even when the ground is waterlogged.

Farming and Food

We could not survive without rainwater. Humans need water not only for drinking and washing, but also for the foods that we eat, which could not exist without water. There is no guarantee that rain will fall just when the crops need it, so in some countries irrigation is essential. That means delivering stored rain or river water to the fields and using pipes and sprayers.

DRESSING FOR DRYNESS

In warmer parts of the world, where rain is eagerly awaited to water the crops, the first drops of the monsoon are greeted by people running outside and dancing until they are drenched. In colder areas, keeping dry is a higher priority, for wet clothes cannot keep our bodies warm. Umbrellas are not very useful in a high wind, or when you need both hands free.

Modern fabrics are made for various kinds of weather. Waterproof clothing will protect you in a light shower, but it becomes soaked in a heavy downpour. Fabrics that are completely waterproof sometimes have holes in them! This is so that while most water is kept out, air can circulate to keep the body from producing more water in the form of sweat.

▲ These cyclists in Shanghai wear capes made from modern lightweight fabrics. They can be folded up and carried.

▲ These traditional "raincoats" in rural India are made of natural materials.

SMELLY, BUT DRY!

★ The earliest way to weatherproof clothes was to rub them with oil or grease. That worked, but was also very smelly! Later, coating fabric with rubber worked even better, but was still quite smelly. Today's artificial fabrics are both waterproof and windproof, as well as being odor-free!

Building Styles

Huge cities often look similar wherever they are, but in the country local materials have to be used to make buildings as weatherproof as possible. In cold areas, steeply pitched roofs help water run away quickly to the ground below. In such places, modern flat roofs have often caused problems. In storm-swept areas, houses may have shutters and porches. Porches stop rain and wind from rushing in when the front door is opened. In places where the wind is particularly wild, you may see rocks and stones placed on the roofs to keep the roof from flying off in a gale!

▼ **These houses on stilts in the Philippines are designed for areas that flood frequently. Belongings are kept a few feet (meters) above the water.**

GETTING AROUND

Imagine icy rain trickling down your neck and savage winds lashing branches into your face. Two hundred years ago, this was the kind of experience a traveler might expect on a wild night. Today, we keep dry while crossing huge distances, but wet and windy weather still affects our travels.

Storms at Sea

Modern ships are no longer at the mercy of the wind and waves as sailing ships once were. They receive regular weather forecasts by radio and fax and have advanced buoyancy and stabilizing systems to help them ride even the highest waves.

Driving in the Rain

Vehicles and roads are designed with wet and windy weather in mind. Roads need good drainage so that surface water will not cause cars to

skid out of control. Modern tires also help throw water to the side, so that the rubber can grip the road beneath. Highways are often protected from cross-winds by high banks and fences. Vehicles traveling at high speeds can literally be blown off course if they are hit by a sudden sideways gust. That is also why long bridges are sometimes closed to high-sided vehicles such as trucks. The wind can blow up a river or estuary, hitting the bridge from the side with enormous force.

▼ Surface water is very dangerous. It can cause vehicles to skid, can hide potholes and road markings, and can freeze into an icy sheet if the temperature drops.

▼ Almost all waves are caused by wind, not by tides.

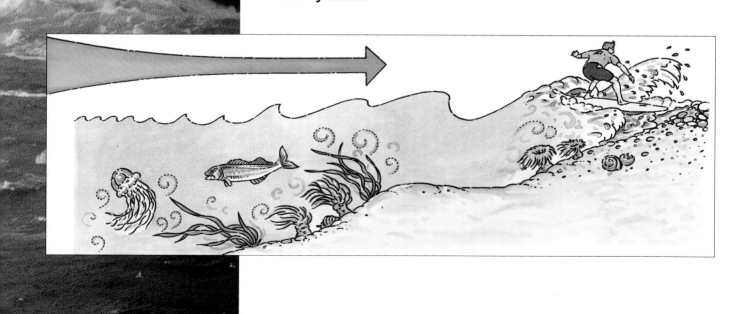

◀ Most sailboats are used for pleasure instead of for transporting goods.

▶ Air movements, or eddies of rising warm air called thermals, can allow a hang glider to swoop for many minutes after being launched from a steep precipice. Birds of prey also use thermals to glide above hills or cliffs.

LEISURE
Luckily, there is a lighter side to wild weather. High winds can provide hours of fun if harnessed in the right way. Some sports would be very difficult to play without the wind!

Wind Power
Sailing, windsurfing, and even kite flying rely on brisk breezes. People skilled in these activities need to understand how to use the wind's power. Sailors, for example, are expert at sailing a zigzag course to reach their destinations, no matter which direction the wind is blowing from.

Speed Skill
Not all wind-powered sports take place at sea. Sand yachts are not boats at all but hulls on wheels with masts and sails. They make full use of sea and land breezes to race along the shore, with the "sailor" lying almost flat beneath the sail. Even more skill is needed for kite yachting, where a kite, instead of a sail, pulls its owner along in a wheeled cart. It's not easy watching the kite and where you are going at the same time! Some daring explorers also use kite technology. Antarctic travelers can travel up to 100 mi. (160 km) a day, pulled by specially designed kites.

DEALING WITH DISASTER

▲ Bad weather can cause problems for rescuers as
well as for those they are rescuing. Helicopters have to
wait until high winds have dropped before they can fly.

Sometimes forecasts and warnings cannot prevent a storm from causing disastrous damage. Then speedy help is absolutely essential.

Being Prepared

When it is known that an area can suffer extreme weather conditions, it is vital to have a plan if the worst happens. Good communications among all the people concerned is the most important thing, but that can be difficult in areas without electricity or radio. It is crucial that everyone know exactly what his or her job is and how to keep in touch with the emergency center coordinating all the activity.

DISASTER PLAN

★ Warn likely victims and emergency services.

★ Assess the situation frequently.

★ Coordinate emergency services to tackle the most urgent problems first.

★ Supply backup to emergency services and victims—medical aid, shelter, food, clothing, information.

★ Develop plans to restore things to normal when the danger has passed.

★ Afterward, consider improvements to the plans for next time.

▲ Time passes slowly for those who have been evacuated from their homes in Wilmington, North Carolina, as they wait for Hurricane Bertha to arrive.

Calling for Help

The manner in which emergency services are called is always changing as more modern methods become available. For example, in the past when a lifeboat had to be launched, crew members were called by ringing the church bells. Later, a special siren was sounded to give a clearer signal. Today, crew members often carry pagers in their pockets.

THE FUTURE

In areas where the weather is very changeable, we often hear people saying, "We've been lucky with the weather," when they simply mean that an outdoor event has gone ahead despite rainy weather. We often think that weather is something that happens to us whether we like it or not. But nowadays we are beginning to see that what human beings do on Earth can change a great deal in the natural world—and that includes the weather.

Natural Energy

By burning fossil fuels and using up our planet's nonrenewable resources, the earth's atmosphere is being changed, and that, after all, is where the weather happens. The challenge now is to make sure that in the future, natural forces and technology are not in conflict.

◄ **Wind farms are a clean and useful source of energy. These tall windmills, which are often found in large groups, drive generators to produce electricity.**

◀ Clouds of air pollution can be carried for hundreds of miles by the wind. Eventually, some kinds of pollution fall to Earth in the form of acid rain, killing trees in forests and fish in lakes.

▼ The world's rain forests are sometimes known as the lungs of the planet. They "breathe" out oxygen and carbon dioxide into the atmosphere. If current rates of destruction continue, the rain forests will disappear by the end of the 21st century.

GLOSSARY

Anemometer An instrument for measuring wind speed.

Anticyclone An area of high atmospheric pressure.

Atmosphere The layer of gases that surrounds our planet, including the air that we breathe.

Atmospheric pressure The pressing down of the atmosphere (or air) upon the earth. Cold air pushes down with a greater pressure than warm air.

Barometer An instrument for measuring atmospheric pressure.

Climate The general weather trends in a particular area.

Cyclone An area of low atmospheric pressure; also the swirling winds that can occur in such an area.

Depression Another word for a cyclone.

Flood Water that arrives too quickly to run into drains and ditches, but instead pools above ground.

Front The line along which a hot air mass and a cold air mass meet.

Hurricane A Force-12 wind on the Beaufort scale.

Meteorology The study of weather and how future weather can be predicted.

Monsoon A wind blowing in South Asia and the prolonged rains that it may bring with it.

Myth A traditional story, usually dealing with powerful or mysterious events and perhaps trying to explain them.

Reservoir A special lake for storing water.

Tornado A violent storm with whirling winds.

Troposphere The lower level of the atmosphere, where our planet's weather takes place.

Typhoon A violent wind in East Asian seas.

MORE OF INTEREST

Books to Read

Bramwell, Martyn. *Weather.* (Earth Science Library.) Danbury, CT: Franklin Watts, 1994.

Catherall, Ed. *Exploring Weather.* (Exploring Science.) Austin, TX: Raintree Steck-Vaughn, 1990.

Cosgrove, Brian. *Weather.* (Eyewitness Books.) New York: Knopf Books for Young Readers, 1991.

Davis, Kay & Oldsfield, Wendy. *The Super Science Book of Weather.* (Super Science.) New York: Thomson Learning, 1993.

Gardner, Robert & Webster, David. *Science Projects about Weather.* (Science Projects.) Springfield, NJ: Enslow Publishers, 1994.

Grumbine, Robert W. *Discover Weather.* (Discover.) Lake Forest, IL: Forest House, 1992.

Kahl, Jonathan. *Weatherwise: Learning about the Weather.* (How's the Weather?) Minneapolis, MN: Lerner Group, 1992.

Kahl, Jonathan. *Wet Weather: Rain Showers & Snowfall.* (How's the Weather?) Minneapolis, MN: Lerner Group, 1992.

Llewellyn, Claire. *Wind & Rain.* (Why Do We Have?) Hauppauge, NY: Barron's Educational Series, Inc., 1995.

Mason, John. *Weather & Climate.* (Our World.) Parsippany, NJ: Silver Burdett Press, 1991.

Steele, Philip. *Rain: Causes & Effects.* (Weather Watch.) Danbury, CT: Franklin Watts, 1991.

Time Life Books Staff. *Weather & Climate.* (Understanding Science & Nature.) Alexandria, VA: Time-Life Inc., 1992.

CD ROMs

Violent Earth (Raintree Steck-Vaughn, 1996)

INDEX

© Copyright 1997 Wayland (Publishers) Ltd.

Picture Acknowledgments
British Sky Broadcasting: 28; Corbis (UK):
43; Frank Lane Pictures: 15, 40/41, 45;
Robert Harding Associates: 4/5, 9, 16/17;
Hutchison Library: 11, 33t, 34/35, 36b;
Panos Pictures: 6, 7, 8, 36t, 37; Popperfoto:
22/23, 33b; Royal Navy: 42; Tony Stone
Associates: 26, 32, 44.